# Funnybone

*You don't stop laughing when you grow old.
You grow old when you stop laughing.*

# Funnybone

*You don't stop laughing when you grow old.*
*You grow old when you stop laughing.*

**Pearce W. Hammond**

**Senilmentia Publishers**
**Okatie, South Carolina**

Senilmentia Publishers
20 Bellinger Cove
Okatie, South Carolina 29909


ISBN-13: 978-1480034624
ISBN-10: 1480034622

Library of Congress Catalog Card Number: 2012918626


Printed in the United States of America



To order for family, friends or colleagues: www.pearcehammond.com

This book is dedicated
to everyone with a Funnybone
who enjoys laughing
and making others laugh.

Large
Type
Edition

# Introduction

As seniors get older, their bodies show signs of aging but they can still stay young at heart by laughing. Laughter is infectious. The sound of roaring laughter is far more contagious than any cough, sniffle or sneeze. When laughter is shared, it binds people together and increases happiness and intimacy. Laughter also triggers healthy physical changes in the body. It strengthens the immune system, boosts energy, dimishes pain, and protects from the damaging effects of stress. Nothing works faster or more dependably than a good laugh to bring your mind and body back into balance. Humor also lightens your burdens, inspires hopes, connects you to others and keeps you grounded, focused and alert.

With so much power to heal and renew,

the ability to laugh easily and frequently is a tremendous resource for surmounting problems, enhancing your relationships, and supporting both physical and emotional health.

Best of all, this priceless medicine is fun, free and easy to use. All you have to do is read this book and let your funnybone do the rest.

*Pearce W. Hammond*
*Author*

**A man walked** into his office one morning with his fly unzipped and wide open. His secretary noticed it and remarked, *"This morning when you left your house, did you remember to close your garage door?"*

Her boss then told her that he knew that he had closed his garage door and walked into his office. As he finished his paperwork, he suddenly noticed that his fly was open and called his secretary into his office and said, *"When my garage door was open, did you see my Hummer parked in there?"* She smiled and said, *"No, all I saw was an old mini van with two flat tires."*

**A wife turned** to her husband and said, *"You don't look anything like the long haired, skinny kid I married 25 years ago. I need a DNA sample to make sure it's still you."*

It's no longer
a question of
staying healthy.
It's a question
of finding a
sickness you
like.

*Jackie Mason*

**Two old women,** Gertrude and Helen, were talking in a nursing home. Gertrude said, *"Barbara has just cremated her sixth husband."*

*"I guess that's the way it goes,"* replied Helen. *"Some of us can't find a husband and others have husbands to burn."*

———————————

**An elderly man** asked his wife if she would like to have some ice cream while they were watching TV. *"Sure"*, she said. *"I'd also like some strawberries on top with some whipped cream and I want you to write this down before you go to the kitchen so you won't forget it."* Irritated, he said: *"I don't need to write it down. I got it. Ice cream with strawberries and whipped cream."* About 30 minutes later when he returned from the kitchen, he hands his wife a plate of scrambled eggs and bacon. She stares at the plate and then says, *"Where's my toast?"*

# Jewelry
# takes
# people's minds
# off your
# wrinkles.

*Sonja Henie*

**An 88 year old** man went to his doctor for a physical. A few days later his doctor saw him walking down the street with a beautiful young chick on his arm. The next day the doctor spoke with him and said, *"You're really doing great, aren't you?"* The man replied: *"Doc, I'm just doing what you told me to do. To go out and get a hot mama and be cheerful."* The doctor then replied: *"I didn't say that. I said, you've got a heart murmur so be careful!"*

---

**An old man** shuffled into an ice cream parlor and slowly and painfully pulled himself up on a stool. After catching his breath, he ordered a banana split. The waitress then said kindly, *"Crushed nuts?"* *"No, replied the old man, I've got Arthritis!"*

**Many people die at twenty-five and aren't buried until they are seventy-five.**

*Benjamin Franklin*

**An old woman** was given a physical exam by her doctor and told that she was in good physical condition for her age. He then asked her: *"Do you still have Intercourse?"* She replied: *"I'll have to check with my husband."*

After reaching her husband on the phone, she turned to the doctor and replied: *"No, we have Blue Cross and Blue Shield."*

---

**To all my** friends and relatives who have sent me best wishes, chain letters, angel letters or other promises of good luck. None of that shit has worked. Could you please send me cash, vodka, chocolate, Italian food, wine, or airline tickets instead?

---

*You Know You're Getting Old When....*

You turn out the lights for economic rather than romantic reasons.

I was thirty-seven when I went to work writing the column.
I was too old for a paper route, too young for Social Security, and too tired for an affair.

*Erma Bombeck*

**Mildred was** a 93 year-old woman who was particularly despondent over the recent death of her husband, Sam. She decided that she would just kill herself and join him in heaven. Thinking that it would be best to get it over with quickly, Mildred took out Sam's old Army pistol and made the decision to shoot herself in the heart since it was so badly broken in the first place. Not wanting to miss the vital organ and become a vegetable and a burden to someone, she called her doctor's office to inquire as to just exactly where the heart was located. *"On a woman,"* the doctor said, *"your heart would be just below your left breast."* Later that night, Mildred was admitted to the hospital with a gunshot wound to her knee.

---

**Ethyl and Mertle** were sitting in a nursing home talking to each other when Ethyl remarked, *"I'm getting so old that all my friends in heaven will think I didn't make it."*

# Sex after ninety is like trying to shoot pool with a rope.

## *George Burns*

**An elderly gentlemen** went to see his doctor and asked for a prescription of Viagra. The doctor said, *"that's no problem. How many do you want?" "Just a few,"* the man remarked, *"but cut each tablet into four pieces."* The doctor replied, *"That won't do you any good."* The elderly gentlemen then said, *"That's all right. I don't need them for sex anymore as I'm over 90 years old. I just want my private to stick out far enough so I don't pee on my shoes."*

---

**An old lady** pulled up to a U.S. Mail box and leaned out the window of her car and said, *"I'll have a Cheeseburger, large fries and black coffee."* One person standing nearby said to another, *"I'm starting to think retesting seniors for a driver's license isn't a bad idea."*

# Do not worry about avoiding temptation. As you grow older, it will avoid you.

*Joey Adams*

**A old couple** had been married for 50 years and were sitting at the breakfast table one morning when the old man said to his wife, *"Just think, honey, we've been married for 50 years."* "Yeah," she replied, *"50 years ago we were sitting here at this breakfast table together."* "I know," the old man said, *"We were probably sitting here naked as jaybirds!"* "Well," his wife snickered, *"What do you say ... should we get naked again?"* The old man nodded, and the two of them took all their clothes off and sat back down at the table. *"You know, honey,"* the old lady whispered breathlessly, *"My nipples are as hot for you today as they were 50 years ago."* *"I wouldn't be surprised,"* replied her husband, *"one's in your coffee and the other's in your oatmeal!"*

---

### *You Know You're Getting Old When....*

You burn the midnight oil until 9pm.

I get up each morning and dust off my wits, then pick up the paper and read the 'o-bits.' If my name isn't there, then I know I'm not dead. I eat a good breakfast and go back to bed.

*- Anonymous*

**An eighty year** old man was sitting on the couch with his wife when she said to him, *"Why don't you come sit close to me like you used to."* So he did. After a moment she said, *"Why don't you put your arm around me like you used to."* He then put his arm around her and held her tight. Then she said, *"Why don't you nibble on my ear like you used to."* The man got up and left the room. *"Where are you going?"* she called out. *"To get my teeth,"* he replied.

━━━━━━━━━━━━━━━━━━━

**I was asleep** and dreaming of the old days of hot-tubs and free sex when all of a sudden the awesome reality of a firm breast in my mouth caused me to slowly rise from my slumber. It turned out to be the rubber nose piece from my CPAP machine which came off and fell into my mouth and I had been chewing on it.

The instructions read, 'Take one pill, three times a day.' How am I supposed to do that? Tie a string to it?

*-Anonymous*

**Two old ladies** were outside their nursing home smoking a cigarette when it started to rain. One of the ladies pulled out a condom, cut off the end, put it over her cigarette and continued smoking.

Lady 1: "*What's that?*"

Lady 2: "*A condom. This way my cigarette doesn't get wet.*"

Lady 1: "*Where did you get it?*"

Lady 2: "*You can get them at any drugstore.*"

The next day lady 1 hobbles herself into the local drugstore and announces to the pharmacist that she wants a box of condoms. The guy looks at her kind of strangely (she is, after all, over 80 years old), but politely asks what brand she prefers.

Lady 1: "*It doesn't matter as long as it fits a Camel.*"

The pharmacist fainted.

# After age 70, it's just patch, patch, patch.

*-Jimmy Stewart*

**An elderly couple** was on a cruise and the water was really rough. They were standing on the back of the ship watching the moon when a wave came up and washed the old woman overboard. They searched and searched, but couldn't find her. The captain sent her husband back to shore with the promise that he would notify him as soon as they found something. Three weeks went by and finally the old man got a fax from the ship. It read: "*Sir, sorry to inform you but we finally found your wife at the bottom of the ocean, and she was dead. As a side issue, the medical examiner found an oyster stuck in her vagina, and inside it was a pearl worth $50,000. Please advise what you want us to do.*" The old man faxed back: "*Send me the pearl and re-bait the trap.*"

The secret to
staying young
is to live
honestly, eat
slowly, and lie
about your age.

*-Licille Ball*

**A little boy** and his grandfather were raking leaves in the yard. The little boy sees an Earthworm trying to get back into its hole. He says, *"Grandpa, I bet I can put that worm back in that hole."* The grandfather replied, *"I'll bet you five bucks you can't. It's too wiggly and limp to put back in that little hole. "*

The little boy runs into the house and comes back out with a can of hairspray. He sprays the worm until it is straight and stiff as a board. Then he stuffs the worm back into the hole. The grandfather hands the little boy five dollars, grabs the hairspray and runs into the house. Thirty minutes later, the grandfather comes back out and hands the little boy another five dollars.

The little boy says, *"Grandpa, you already gave me five bucks."* The grandfather replies, *"I know. That's from your grandma."*

You can be
young without
money
but you can't
be old
without it.


-*Tennessee Williams*

# You're Getting Old When . . .

One of the throw pillows on your bed is a hot water bottle.

Dinner and a movie is the entire date instead of the beginning of one.

At the breakfast table you hear snap, crackle, pop and you're not eating cereal.

The waiter asks how you would like your steak and you say *"Pureed!"*

You sit in a rocking chair and can't get it going.

You wake up looking like your driver's license picture.

Your secrets are safe with your friends because they can't remember them either.

# The three immutable facts:
# You own stuff.
# You will die.
# Someone will get that stuff.

*-Jane Bryant Quinn*

**Miss Charlotte** was in her 80's and the pastor came to call on her one afternoon. She welcomed him into her Victorian parlour and invited him to have a seat while she prepared a little tea. As he sat facing her old pump organ, he noticed a crystal glass bowl sitting on top of it filled with water. In the water floated, of all things, a condom.

When Miss Charlotte returned with tea and cookies, they began to chat. The pastor tried to stifle his curiosity about the bowl and its strange floater, but soon it got the best of him, and he could resist no longer.

*"Miss Charlotte,"* he said, *"I wonder if you would tell me about this,* pointing to the bowl. *"Oh, yes,"* she replied, *"Isn't it wonderful? I was walking downtown last fall and I found this little package. It said to put it on your organ and keep it wet, and it would prevent disease. And you know, I think it is working. I haven't had a cold all winter!"*

When grace is
joined with
wrinkles,
it is adorable.
There is an
unspeakable
dawn in
happy
old age.

*-Victor Hugo*

**An old man** and his wife went to bed and after laying there a few minutes the old man farts and says, *"Seven Points."* His wife rolls over and says, *"What in the world was that?"* The old man replied, *"It's fart football... I just scored."*

A few minutes later the wife lets one go and says, *"Touchdown, tie score."*

After about five minutes, the old man farts again and says, *"Touchdown, I'm ahead 14 to 7."*

Not to be out done, the wife rips another one and says, *"Touchdown, tie score."* Five seconds go by and she lets out a squeaker and says, *"Field goal, I lead 17 to 14."* Now the pressure's on and the old man refuses to get beat by a woman so he strains real hard but to no avail. Realizing a defeat is totally unacceptable, he gives it everything he has, but instead of farting, he poops in the bed. The wife looks and says, *"What the heck was that?"* The old man replied, *"Half-time, Switch sides."*

You don't get
to choose how
you are going
to die.
Or when.
You can only
decide how
you are going
to live. Now

*-Joan Baez*

# 10 Games for Old People

**1.** 20 Questions shouted in your good ear.

**2.** Pin the Toupee on the bald guy.

**3.** Sag, You're it.

**4.** Kick the bucket.

**5.** Doc Goose

**6.** Red Rover, Red Rover, the nurse says Bend Over.

**7.** Hide and go pee.

**8.** Simon says something incoherent.

**9.** Musical recliners

**10.** Spin the bottle of Mylanta.

---

It's amazing... according to the obituary column in the newspaper, people die in alphabetical order.

# Half our life is spent trying to find something to do with the time we have rushed through life trying to save.

*-Will Rogers*

**I've sure gotten old!** I've had two bypass surgeries, a hip replacement, new knees, fought prostate cancer and diabetes. I'm half blind, can't hear anything quieter than a jet engine, take 40 different medications that make me dizzy, winded, and subject to blackouts. Have bouts with dementia. Have poor circulation and hardly feel my hands and feet anymore. Can't remember if I'm 88 or 94. Have lost all my friends. But, thank God, I still have my driver's license.

———————————

**Two elderly gentlemen** from a retirement center were sitting on a bench under a tree when one turned to the other and said: *"Slim, I'm 86 years old now and I'm just full of aches and pains. I know you're about my age. How do you feel?"* Slim replied, *"I feel just like a newborn baby. "Really!? Like a newborn baby?" "Yep. No hair, no teeth, and I think I just wet and pooped in my pants."*

I knew a man who gave up smoking, drinking, sex, and food. He was healthy right up to the time he killed himself.

-*Johnny Carson*

**An elderly gentleman** had serious hearing problems for a number of years. He went to the doctor and the doctor was able to have him fitted for a set of hearing aids that allowed him to hear 100%. He went back in a month and the doctor said, *"Your hearing is perfect. Your family must be really pleased that you can hear again."* The gentleman replied, *"Oh, I haven't told my family yet. I just sit around and listen to the conversations and I've changed my will three times!"*

---

**On his deathbed,** a husband gasped weakly to his wife, *"Please, my dear, I want you to grant me one last wish before I die."* *"What is it?"* she asked. *"Six months after I die I want you to marry Bob from next door."* *"But I thought you hated Bob,"* she said. *"I do,"* said the husband.

# Middle age is when your age starts to show around your middle.

*-Bob Hope*

**Two senior citizens** are pushing their carts around Walmart, looking left and right, when they collide head-on. The first guy says to the second guy, *"Sorry about that. I'm looking for my wife, and I guess I wasn't paying attention to where I was going."* The second old guy says, *"That's OK, it's a coincidence. I'm looking for my wife, too. I can't find her and I'm getting a little desperate."* The first old guy says, *"Well, maybe I can help you find her. What does she look like?"* *"Well, she is 27 yrs old, tall, with red hair, blue eyes, long legs, and is wearing short shorts. What does your wife look like?"* *"She can wait. Let's look for yours."*

---

**Alice was asked** by a friend if she ever thinks about the hereafter. She said, *"I do all the time. No matter where I am in the house - kitchen, den, upstairs, downstairs and then I ask myself......now what am I here after?"*

43

I am ready to meet my Maker. Whether my Maker is prepared for the ordeal of meeting me is another matter.

-*Winston Churchill*

**A senior citizen** said to his eighty-year old buddy: *"So I hear you're getting married?"* *"Yep!"* *"Do I know her?"* *"Nope!"* *"This woman...is she good looking?"* *"Not really."* *"Is she a good cook?"* *"No, she can't cook very well."* *"Does she have lots of money?"* *"Nope! She's poor as a church mouse."* *"Well, then, is she good in bed?"* *"I don't know."* *"Why in the world do you want to marry her then?"* *"Because she can still drive after dark!"*

---

**An elderly couple** went to church one Sunday and halfway through the service, the wife leans over and whispers in her husbands ear, *"I've just cut a silent fart. What do you think I should do?"* The husband quickly responds, *"Put a new battery in your hearing aid."*

Grow up,
and that is a
terribly hard
thing to do.
It is much easier
to skip it and go
from one
childhood to
another.

*-F. Scott Fitzgerald*

**Three old women** are talking about their aches, pains and bodily dysfunctions. One seventy-eight year old woman says, "*I have this problem. I wake up every morning at seven and it takes me twenty minutes to pee.*"

An eighty seven year old woman then says, "*My case is worse. I get up at eight and I sit there and grunt and groan for half an hour before I finally have a bowel movement.*"

The ninety six year old woman then says, "*At seven I pee like a horse, at eight I crap like a cow.*"

"*So what's your problem?*" asked the others. "*I don't wake up until nine.*"

---

**Did you hear** about the three elderly men who hijacked a truck full of Viagra?

The police are looking for an old gang of hardened criminals.

47

# Learning and sex until rigor mortis.

*-Maggie Kuhn*

**A dying man,** who had no surviving family members, called his accountant to his deathbed. *"When I die,"* he told his accountant, *"I want you to have my remains cremated."*
*"And what would you like me to do with your ashes?"* asked his accountant.
The old man replied, *"Put them in an envelope and mail them to the IRS with a note saying now you have everything!"*

---

**As a senior citizen** was driving down the freeway when his car phone rang. Answering, he heard his wife's voice urgently warning him, *"John, I just heard on the news that there's a car going the wrong way on Interstate 77. Please be careful!"* "Heck", said John, *"It's not just one car. It's hundreds of them!"*

---

### You Know You're Getting Old When....

Your train of thought frequently derails.

I have long thought that the aging process could be slowed down if it had to work its way through Congress.

*-George H. W. Bush*

**An elderly couple** was sitting together watching television. During a commercial, the husband asked his wife, *"Whatever happened to our sexual relations?"* After a long thoughtful silence and during the next commercial, the wife replied, *"You know, I don't know. I don't even think we got a Christmas card from them this year."*

**At age 4,** success is not peeing in your pants.

**At age 12,** success is having friends.

**At age 16,** success is having a drivers license.

**At age 20,** success is having sex.

**At age 35,** success is having money.

**At age 50,** success is having money.

**At age 60,** success is having sex.

**At age 70,** success is having a drivers license.

**At age 75,** success is having friends.

**At age 80,** success is not peeing in your pants.

# The Trouble with class reunions is that old flames have become even older.

*-Doug Larson*

**A little old lady** was running up and down the halls in a nursing home. As she walked, she would flip up the hem of her nightgown and say *"Supersex."* Walking up to an elderly man in a wheelchair and flipping up her gown at him, she said, *"Supersex."* He sat silently for a moment or two and finally answered, *"I'll take the soup."*

━━━━━━━━━━

**The rescue squad** was called to the home of an elderly couple for a heart attack the gentleman was having. When the squad got there, it was too late and the man had died. While consoling the wife, one of the rescuers noticed that the bed was a mess. He asked the lady what symptoms the man had suffered and if anything had precipitated the heart attack. The lady replied, *"Well, we were in the bed making love when he started moaning, groaning, thrashing about the bed, panting, and sweating. I thought he was coming - but I guess he was going."*

# Older women are best because they always think they may be doing it for the last time.

*-Ian Fleming*

**When the husband** finally died his wife put the usual death notice in the paper, but added that he died of Gonorrhea. No sooner were the papers delivered, when one of the children called and complained bitterly, *"You know very well that dad died of Diarrhea, not Gonorrhea."* The widowed mother replied, *"I nursed him night and day, so of course I know that he died of Diarrhea. But I thought it would be better for posterity to remember him as a great lover rather than as the big self-serving shit head that he always was."*

---

**Bill's friends** say he has a photographic memory. However, most of the time he forgets to take the lens cap off.

---

*You Know You're Getting Old When....*
You need glasses to find your glasses.

Put cotton in your ears and pebbles in your shoes. Pull on rubber gloves. Smear Vasoline over your glasses, and there you have it: instant old age.

-*Malcolm Cowley*

**Two old women** were discussing their husbands over tea. *"I wish that my Harry would stop biting his nails. It gets me very upset."*

*"My Calvin used to do the same thing,"* the other old woman replied. *"But I broke him of the habit." "How?"* the first women asked, *"I hid his teeth."*

---

**I cannot see.** I cannot pee. I cannot chew. I cannot screw. My memory shrinks. My hearing stinks. No sense of smell and I look like hell. How did it get so late so soon? It's night before it's afternoon, and December is here before its June. My goodness how the time has flown. The Golden Years have come at last. The Golden Years can kiss my ass.

---

*You Know You're Getting Old When....*

You and your teeth don't sleep together.

# Retirement must be wonderful. I mean, you can suck in your stomach for only so long.

*-Burt Reynolds*

**A man** was out walking one day and went by a retirement home. As he passed the front lawn, he saw nine old ladies basking in the sun in lounge chairs. When he looked closer, he realized that they were all buck naked. He went to the door and rang the bell. When the director answered the door, the man asked if he realized there were nine naked old ladies lying in the sun on the front lawn. The director said, "*Yes*" and went on to explain that the old ladies were all retired prostitutes living at the retirement home, and were having a yard sale.

An elderly lady who lived in the country drove into town to buy 10 yards of outing flannel to make a nightgown. The clerk asked her why she needed to buy 10 yards. The old lady replied, "*My husband has more fun hunting for it than when he finds it.*"

# To me, old age is always fifteen years older than I am.

*-Bernard Baruch*

**The woman stopped** by her son's house. She rang the doorbell, stepped into the house, and saw her daughter-in-law standing naked by the door. *"What are you doing?"* she asked. *"I'm waiting for your son to come home from work,"* she said. *"But you're naked!"* exclaimed her mother-in-law. *"This is my Love Dress."* the daughter-in-law remarked. *"Love Dress? But you're naked!"* *"My husband loves me to wear this dress. It makes him happy and it makes me happy. I would appreciate it if you would leave because he will be home from work any minute."* The mother-in-law was tired of hearing all of this and left and thought about the Love Dress on the way home. When she got home, she got buck naked, put on her best perfume and waited by the front door. When her husband got home from work and saw her standing naked by the door, he said, *"What are you doing?"* *"This is My Love Dress,"* she replied. *"Needs ironing."* he said.

I think all this
talk about age
is foolish.
Every time I'm
one year older,
everyone else is
too.

*-Gloria Swanson*

**Elvira loves** to charge down the long corridors at the nursing home in her wheel chair. Everybody tolerates it and some of the men have actually been known to join in. The other day, Elvira was speeding up a corridor when a door opened and Mad Mike stepped out of his room with his arm outstretched, "*STOP!*" he demanded. *"Have you got a license for that thing?"* Elvira fished around in her handbag and pulled out a candy wrapper and held it up to him. "*OK*" he said, and away she sped down the hall. As she passed by the TV lounge, crazy Charles popped his head out and shouted, "*STOP! Have you got proof of insurance?*" Elvira dug into her handbag, pulled out a beer coaster and held it up to him. Charles nodded and said, *"Carry on, baby."* As she neared another corridor before the front door, Boozer Bob stepped out in front of her, stark naked, holding a huge erection in his hand. *"Oh, no!"* said Elvira, *"Not the Breathalyzer again!"*

# Old age is no place for sissies.

*-Bette Davis*

**Mr. Smith,** an old man, resided in a nursing home. One day he went into the nurses' office and informed Nurse Ratchett that his penis had died. Nurse Ratchett, realizing that Mr. Smith was old and somewhat senile, decided to play along with him. *"It did? I'm sorry to hear that,"* she replied. Two days later, Mr. Smith was walking up and down the halls at the nursing home with his penis hanging outside of his pants. Nurse Ratchett saw him and said, *"Mr. Smith, I thought you told me that your penis had died."* "It did," he replied, *"Today is the viewing."*

---

## *You Know You're Getting Old When....*

Getting a little action means you don't have to take a laxative.

Life would be infinitely happier if we could only be born at the age of eighty and gradually approach eighteen.

-*Mark Twain*

**An old man** and his wife went to the doctor for a check-up. While the man is with the doctor, the doctor asks him, *"So how has life been treating you?"* The old man replies, *"The Lord's been good to me. Every night when I go to the bathroom, he turns the light on and when I'm finished, he turns the light off."* While the old man's wife is with the doctor, the doctor told her what her husband had said and she replied, *"Damn it! The old fart's been pissing in the ice box again!"*

---

Just before the funeral services, the undertaker came up to the very elderly widow and asked, *"How old was your husband?"* *"98,"* she replied, *"Two years older than me."* *"So you're 96,"* the undertaker commented. She responded, *"Hardly worth going home, is it?"*

Don't worry about senility, my grandfather use to say. 'When it hits you, you won't know it.'

-Bill Cosby

**An old lady** was standing at the railing of the cruise ship holding her hat on tight, so that it would not blow off in the wind. A gentleman approached her and said: *"Pardon me, madam. I do not intend to be forward, but did you know that your dress is blowing up in this high wind?"* *"Yes, I know,"* she said, *"I need both hands to hold onto this hat."* *"But, madam, you must know that your privates are exposed"*, said the gentleman in earnest. The woman looked down, then back up at the man and replied, *"Sir, anything you see down there is 91 years old. I just bought this hat yesterday!"*

---

**An elderly man** went to see his doctor for consultation over some lab tests. *"I've got good news and bad news,"* said the doctor. *"The good news is you only have 24 hours to live."* *"Wow"*, said the patient, *"If that's the good news then what is the bad news?"* The doctor replied, *"I forgot to call you yesterday!"*

Men are like
wine. Some
turn to vinegar,
but the best
improve
with age.

*-Pope John XXIII*

**An old lady** walked into a bar on a cruise ship and ordered Scotch with two drops of water. As the bartender poured it, she revealed that it was her eightieth birthday. Hearing this, a fellow passenger offered to buy her a drink. *"Thank you,"* she said. *"How kind. I'll have another Scotch with two drops of water."*

The bartender was impressed by her drinking capacity but wondered why she only asked for two drops of water in her drink.

*"Well,"* she explained, *"when you've reached my age, you've learned how to hold your liquor. But water is a different matter."*

---

**Reporters interviewing** a 104-year-old woman: *"What do you think is the best thing about being 104?"* the reporter asked. She simply replied, *"No peer pressure."*

# Old age isn't so bad when you consider the alternative.

*-Maurice Chevalier*

## THE SENILITY PRAYER

Grant me the senility to forget the people I never liked anyway, the good fortune to run into the ones I do, and the eyesight to tell the difference.

## My Life Broken Down into Segments

Sleeping...................40%

Working.................2%

Eating....................8%

Looking for things
I had just a minute ago.......50%

# Inside every seventy-year-old is a thirty-five-year-old asking, 'What happened?'

*-Ann Landers*

**An old lady** always held her husband's penis while they were in the recreation room of a nursing home. One day she went down to the recreation room and was shocked to see another women holding his penis. *"What's she got that I don't have"* she asked her husband. He looked up with a large smile on his face and replied: *"Parkinson's."*

---

**An elderly couple** walked into a doctor's office and said they wanted to have a baby. *"At your age,"* the doctor said, *"I don't think it's possible, but I'll give you a jar and come back in a few days with a sperm sample."*

A few days later, the couple returned with an empty jar. *"I was afraid of this,"* the doctor said. *"No, it's not what you think,"* the man said. *"I tried it with my left hand and with my right hand. She tried it with her left and right hand and with her teeth in and with her teeth out but we couldn't get the lid off the jar."*

Middle age is when your old classmates are so gray and wrinkled and bald they don't recognize you.

-Bennett Cerf

**An elderly woman** entered a large furniture store and was greeted by a much young salesman.

*"Is there something in particular I can show you?"* he asked. *"Yes, I want to buy a sexual sofa,"* the old lady replied.

*"You mean a sectional sofa,"* the young salesman suggested.

*"Sectional schmectional"* she bitterly replied. *"All I want is an occasional piece in the living room!"*

---

**An old lady's** two cats died within a few weeks of each other. Finding the house empty without them, she decided to take their bodies to a taxidermist so that they could be put on display in her living room. *"These are my two cats,"* she told the taxidermist. *"They use to be such good friends."* *"That's nice,"* said the taxidermist. *"Tell me do you want them stuffed and mounted?"* *"No,"* replied the old lady, *"Just holding hands."*

Retirement
at 65
is ridiculous.
When I was
sixty-five,
I still had
pimples.

-*George Burns*

**Benefits of having alzheimer's disease**

**1.** You never have to watch reruns on TV.

**2.** You are always meeting new people.

**3.** You don't have to remember the whines and complaints of your spouse.

**4.** You can hide your own Easter eggs.

**5.** Mysteries are always interesting.

---

**Nothing Wrong with My Hearing**

Three retirees, each with a hearing loss, were playing golf one day. One remarked to the other, *"Windy, isn't it?"* *"No,"* the second man replied, *"it's Thursday."* And the third man chimed in, *"So am I. Let's have a beer."*

---

**Two old friends** are talking and one says to the other, *"Did you know that the second thing to go is your memory."* His friend asks, *"What's the first?"* *"I forgot!"*

# Gray hair is God's graffiti.

## -Bill Cosby

**The phone rings** and the lady of the house answers, *"Hello"*. *"Mrs. Smith, please." "Speaking." "Mrs. Smith, this is Doctor Jones at the Medical Testing Laboratory. When your doctor sent your husband's biopsy to the lab yesterday, a biopsy from another Mr. Smith arrived as well, and we are now uncertain which one is your husband's. Frankly, the results are either bad or terrible."*

*"What do you mean?"* Mrs. Smith asks nervously. *"Well, one of the specimens tested positive for Alzheimer's and the other one tested positive for AIDS. We can't tell which is your husband's." "That's dreadful! Can't you do the test again?"* questioned Mrs. Smith. *"Normally we can, but Medicare will only pay for these expensive tests one time." "Well, what am I supposed to do now?" "The people at Medicare recommend that you drop your husband off somewhere in the middle of town. If he finds his way home, don't sleep with him."*

# The best age is the age you are.

*-Maggie Kuhn*

**A woman's husband dies.** He had left $30,000 to be used for an elaborate funeral. After everything is done at the funeral home and cemetery, she tells her closest friend that *"there is absolutely nothing left from the $30,000."* The friend asks, *"How can that be?"* The widow says, *"Well, the funeral cost was $6,500. And of course I made a donation to the church. That was $500, and I spent another $500 for the wake, food and drinks. The rest went for the memorial stone."* The friend says, *"$22,500 for the memorial stone? My God, how big is it?"* The widow says, *"Four and a half carats."*

---

**"Look at me"** an elderly Yuppie boasted to his guests at his birthday bash. *"I've aged like a fine old carefully stored wine."*

*"I certainly have to agree with that,"* replied his obviously long suffering wife. *"Henry's cork has been stationary for years."*

# If you pull out a gray hair, seven will come to its funeral.

*-Pennsylvania German proverb*

**An old lady** lived by herself in a small house in a small town. One day she went to the local grocery store and, while she was gone, a criminal broke into her house, took her clothes off of the line, smashed the watermellons in her garden, shaved her cat and then left when he couldn't find any money. A couple of hours later the old lady got home and when she saw what had happened to her house, she immediately called the police. When the officer answered the phone and asked her what the problem was, she simply replied, *"Someone broke into my house, took my clothes off, squeezed my melons, and shaved my pussy."*

---

**Getting old** is so hard at times. Yesterday I got Preparation 'H' mixed up with Poli-Grip.

# After thirty, a body has a mind of its own.

*-Bette Midler*

**Three older ladies** were discussing the travails of getting older. One said, *"Sometimes I catch myself with a jar of mayonnaise in my hand in front of the refrigerator and can't remember whether I need to put it away, or start making a sandwich."* The second lady chimed in, *"Yes, sometimes I find myself on the landing of the stairs and can't remember whether I was on my way up or on my way down."* The third one responded, *"Well, I'm glad I don't have that problem...knock on wood!"* as she rapped her knuckles on the table, then told them, *"That must be the door, I'll get it!"*

━━━━━━━━━━━━━━━━━

**At his 103rd** birthday party, my grandfather was asked if he planned to be around for his 104th.

*"I certainly do,"* he replied. *"Statistics show that very few people die between the ages of 103 and 104."*

Middle age is when you're faced with two temptations and you choose the one that will get you home by nine o'clock.

-*Ronald Reagan*

**Myrtle is 94 years old** and is angry and phones the newspaper office and loudly demands to know why she never received her Sunday newspaper. *"Ma'am,"* said the employee, *"Today is Saturday and the Sunday paper is not delivered until Sunday."* There was a long pause on the other end of the phone then Myrtle said: *"I'll bet that's why no one was in church today."*

---

**A distraught senior citizen** phoned her doctor's office. *"Is it true,"* she wanted to know, *"that the medication you prescribed has to be taken for the rest of my life?"* *"Yes, I'm afraid so,"* the doctor told her. There was a moment of silence before the senior lady replied, *"I'm wondering, then, just how serious is my condition because this prescription is marked NO REFILLS."*

Beauty comes
in all ages,
colors, shapes,
and forms.
God never
makes junk.

*-Kathy Ireland*

**An elderly woman** went into the doctor's office. When the doctor asked why she was there, she replied, *"I'd like to have some birth control pills."* Taken back, the doctor thought for a minute and then said, *"Excuse me, Mrs. Smith, but you're 78 years old. What possible use could you have for birth control pills?"* The woman responded, *"They help me sleep better."* The doctor thought some more and continued, *"How in the world do birth control pills help you to sleep?"* The woman replied, *"I put them in my granddaughter's orange juice and I sleep better at night."*

---

**My neighbor** who is 98 years old asked me the other day, *"When do you think I should stop saving for my old age."*

---

**Joanne and Henry.** Joanne: *"You know what the problem with getting old is Henry?"* *"No, what's the problem?"* Joanne, *"What problem?"*

# I think of myself as I was twenty-five years ago. Then I look in a mirror and see an old bastard and I realize it's me.

*-Dave Allen*

# Letter from a Mother to her Son

Dear Son:

Just a few lines to let you know that I'm still alive. I'm writing this letter slowly because I know you can't read fast. You won't recognize the house......we've moved. About your father, he has a new job. He has 500 people under him. He's cutting grass at the cemetery. There was a washing machine in the new house when we moved in but it isn't working too good. Last week I put 14 of your father's shirts in it, pulled the handle, and haven't seen the shirts since. Your sister, Mary, had a baby this morning. I haven't found out what it is yet so I don't know whether you're an aunt or an uncle. It only rained twice last week. First for three days, and then again for four days.

Your Loving mother,

*P.S. I was going to send you $10.00 but I had already sealed the envelope.*

93

# Old people shouldn't eat health foods. They need all the preservatives they can get.

*-Robert Orben*

**86-year old Mary** bursts into the recreation room at the retirement home. She holds her clenched fist in the air and announces, *"If anyone here can guess what's in my hand, they can have wild sex with me tonight!!"* An elderly gentleman in the rear says, *"It's an elephant?"* Mary thinks for a minute and then shouts out, *"Close enough."*

---

**An elderly woman** called 911 on her cell phone to report that her car had been broken into. She was hysterical as she explained her situation to the dispatcher: *"They've stolen the stereo, the steering wheel, the brake pedal and even the accelerator!"* she cried.

The dispatcher said, *"Stay calm. An officer is on the way."* A few minutes later, the officer radios in, *"Disregard,"* he says, *"She got in the back-seat by mistake."*

They tell you
that you'll lose
your mind when
you grow older.
What they don't
tell you is that
you won't miss
it much.

*-Malcolm Cowley*

**An 86 year old man** went to a whore house to get his tubes cleaned out. He went back to one of the rooms to await his five minute delight and before the whore entered the room, the old man proceeded to put on a rubber and then took a clothespin and put it on his nose and put ear plugs in his ears. When the whore entered the room and saw the man and what he had done, she said, *"Why have you got that clothespin on your nose and those plugs in your ears?"*

The old man replied, *"Honey, I hate the smell of burning rubber and I'd hate to hear you scream!"*

---

## *You Know You're Getting Old When....*

You realize that a stamp today costs more than a picture show did when you were growing up.

# Wrinkles are hereditary. Parents get them from their children.

*-Doris Day*

**An 80 year old** man picked a new primary care physician. After two visits and many lab tests, the doctor told him he was doing "fairly well" for his age. A little concerned about that comment, the man couldn't resist asking the doctor, "*Do you think I'll live to be 90?*" The doctor replied, "*Do you smoke tobacco or drink whiskey, beer or wine?*" "*Oh no,*" he replied. "*I'm also not doing drugs, either.*" The doctor then asked, "*Do you eat steaks and barbecued ribs? "No, my other Doctor told me that all red meat is very unhealthy." "Do you spend a lot of time in the sun....playing golf, sailing, hiking, or bicycling?" "No, I don't," the man said. "Do you gamble, drive fast cars, fly airplanes or have a lot of sex?" "No,*" he said. "*I don't do any of those things.*" The doctor then looked at him and said, "*Then why do you give a damn whether you make it to 90 or not!*"

# If you live long enough, you're revered rather like an old building.

## -Katharine Hepburn

# How to Stay Young and Happy

**Throw out all the nonessential numbers.** This includes age, weight and height. Let the doctor worry about them. That is why you pay him.

**Keep only cheerful friends.** The grouches pull you down. If you really need a grouch, there are probably a few of your relatives to do the job.

**Keep Learning.** Learn more about the computer, crafts, gardening, whatever. Just never let your brain idle.

**Laugh often, long and loud.** Laugh until you gasp for breath. Laugh so much that you can be tracked in the store by your distinctive laughter.

**Tears happen.** Endure, grieve and move on. The only person who is with you your entire life is yourself.

**Surround yourself with what you love,** whether it is family, pets, keepsakes, music, plants, hobbies, whatever. Your home is your refuge.

**Cherish your health.** If it is good, preserve it. If it is unstable, improve it. If it is beyond what you can improve, get help.

**Don't take guilt trips.** Go to the mall, the next county, a foreign country but not to guilt.

**Tell the people you love that you love them** at every opportunity.

You know
you're old
when you've
lost all your
marvels.

*-Merry Browne*

**An old man named Nathan** had just fallen off of a 2,000 ft. cliff and on his way down grabbed on to a limb about 1,000 ft. from the ground. As he dangled on the limb he yelled out: *"Lord save me...save me. Please Lord save me."* And then a voice came from a cloud floating by and said to him...."*Nathan, this is the Lord. Do you believe in me and do you read the Bible and attend church?"* And Nathan replied: *"Oh, yes, Lord, I read the Bible every day and I go to church 7 days a week."* The lord then said: *"Do you really want to be saved, Nathan?"* And Nathan replied: *"I do, I do, please Lord save me!"* The Lord then said: *"Nathan, will you do anything I say?".* "Oh yes, Lord, I'll do anything you say, just save me." The Lord replied: *"Then Nathan, let go of that limb!"*

Nathan quickly replied, *"BULL SHIT!"*

# *You're Getting Old When . . .*

Happy hour is a nap.

It takes twice as long to look half as good.

People call at 9pm and ask, "Did I wake you?"

Getting a little action means you don't have to take a laxative.

An 'all nighter' means not getting up to pee.

It's tougher to lose weight because over time your body and your fat have become really good friends.

Everything hurts and what doesn't hurt, doesn't work.

You and your teeth don't sleep together.

You can live without sex, but not without glasses.

The pharmacist has become your best friend.

You find yourself standing in line and can't remember why.

You go from hoping for a BMW to hoping for a BM.

You have more hair growing out of your ears than you have on your head.

You learn where your Prostate is.

You look for your glasses for half an hour when they were on your head the whole time.

You realize you've reached your sexpiration date.

You read the obituaries each day to make sure you're not listed.

Your 'get-up-and-go' got up and went.

Your back goes out more than you do.

Your mind writes checks your body can't cover.

Your train of thought frequently derails.

The gleam in your eye is the sun shining on your bifocals.

Your joints are more accurate than the National Weather Service.

You get winded playing cards.

Your pacemaker makes the garage door go up when you see a pretty girl.

Your supply of brain cells is finally down to a manageable size.

A dripping tap causes an uncontrollable urge.

You need glasses to find your glasses.

Things you buy now won't wear out.

Your knees buckle but your belt won't.

Your eyes won't get much worse.

It takes longer to rest than it did to get tired.

Getting lucky means finding your car in a parking lot.

# True Love

**On their 30th** wedding anniversary, a wife turned to her husband and said: *"Will you still love me when my hair has gone grey?"*

*"Why not?"* he replied. *"Haven't I loved you through seven other colors?"*

---

**A woman** who had been raped was in court telling the court what had happened. *"Judge, it happened this way"*, she said. *"I was just walking down the side walk minding my own business when this man came up behind me and pushed me in the bushes and accousted me."* The Judge then replied, *"When he pushed you in the bushes, did you yell for help?"* *"Yeah, Judge, I show did yell for help,"* said the woman. The Judge then questioned her further, *"Well, did anybody come?"* And the woman quickly replied: *"Yeah, Judge, we both did!"*

**A woman named Ruby** was in court charged with murdering her husband with an Ice Pick. The Judge was questioning her. *"Ruby, tell the court what happened."* *"Well Judge, it happened this way. I was in the kitchen just minding my own business when he came up behind me and began tickling me while I was washing my Ice Pick. This frightened me and when I turned around, I accidently stabbed him with the Ice Pick."* And the Judge replied: *"22 times!"*

---

**Mid-life is** when you go to the doctor and you realize you are now so old you have to pay someone to look at you naked.

---

**A senior citizen** went to see his doctor with a complaint that he was unable to perform as a husband. After a cursory exam, the doctor asked how old he was? *"Eighty-six,"* he replied. *"When did you first notice the problem?"* asked the doctor. *"Last night, and it was the same way again this morning!"*

**Two old ladies** were having coffee and were talking about their husbands. As the conversation turned to sex, one old lady asked the other, *"Can your Harry still perform in bed?"* *"He makes me feel like an exercise bike,"* the other lady replied. *"How's that?"* *"He climbs on and starts pumping away but we never get anywhere."*

---

**A group of men** were playing cards when one of them said to the others, *"Let me ask you something. If you could be any type of animal on this Earth, what would you be."* One man replied: *"I'd be a Lion because he's King of the Jungle and a real bad dude."* Another man then stood up and said, *"I've got one that is much better and more practical than a lion. I'd be one of those giant Whales in the sea because that dude has a 10ft. long tongue and he breathes through the top of his head."*

**A man went** to his family doctor and told him that he had a real bad problem. "*Well, what is it?*", said the doctor. "*Well, it's this way*", the man said, "*When I'm making love with my wife, sometimes I can't see and sometimes I can't breathe.*" The doctor then scratched his head and said: "*That's bad. Describe more to me so that I can make a diagnosis.*" "*Well, Doc, when I get my tongue half way in, I can't see, and when I get it all the way in, I can't breathe!*"

---

**An old man** was telling a friend at the nursing home about his new and very expensive hearing aid. "*It's the best on the market,*" he said, "*and it wasn't cheap but it was worth every penny. I can hear so much better now.*" "*What kind is it?*" asked his friend. "*Half past three.*"

**A theatre usher** was alarmed to see an elderly gentlemen crawling on his hands and knees beneath a row of auditorium seats in the middle of a serious dramatic play.

"*What are you doing, sir?*" he whispered. "*You're disturbing the audience around you!*"

"*I've lost my gum,*" answered the old man, continuing to search under the seats.

"*Sir,*" continued the usher, "*If that's your only problem, allow me to offer you another stick of gum so that you can sit down and watch the rest of the play. A stick of gum is not worth all this trouble and commotion.*"

"*But you don't understand,*" said the old man. "*My false teeth are in that gum!*"

**Two elderly gentlemen** were sitting down to breakfast. One said to the other, *"Do you know you've got a suppository in your right ear?"*

*"Speak up. I can't hear you. My hearing aid is not working,"* the other man bellowed.

The first man tapped his ear and pointed to his companion who then delved in his ear and removed a suppository.

*"Im glad you pointed that out. Now I think I know where I put my hearing aid."*

---

**An elderly couple** were sitting on the beach. The old lady turned to her husband and said, *"What do you think of my flip-flops?"*

*"Act your age,"* he replied, *"and put your bikini top back on."*

**An old man** went to see his doctor. *"I need your help, doctor,"* he said. *"Whenever I make love to my wife, my legs go weak at the knees, my head starts spinning, and I have trouble catching my breath. I think it could be something serious."*

*"Well,"* said the doctor, *"I'm afraid your type of symptoms can happen during sex as you get older. By the way, how old are you?"* *"Ninety-Seven,"* the old man replied.

*"And when did you first notice these symptoms?"* asked the doctor.

The old man replied, *"Four times last night and three times this morning."*

---

### *You Know You're Getting Old When....*

You shop for health insurance the way you once shopped for a new car.

**An old man** attended a school reunion but found that his surviving classmates only wanted to talk about their various ailments - heart conditions, liver problems, kidney stones, and other conditions. When he got back home, his wife asked how the reunion went. *"It wasn't so much a school reunion,"* he said, *"It was more like an organ recital!"*

---

**An elderly man** returned from the hospital looking worried. *"What's the matter?"* asked his wife.

*"The consultant said I need to take one of these tablets every day for the rest of my life,"* the husband replied.

*"That's not too bad,"* his wife said, trying to cheer him up.

*"Yes it is,"* said her husband. *"He only gave me seven tablets!"*

**Sam and Bob** were walking down the hall in their nursing home when one of the female residents suddenly ran past them buck naked.

*"Was that Ruth?"* asked Sam.

*"I couldn't be too sure,"* replied Bob. *"My eyesight's not so good these days."*

*"Neither is mine,"* agreed Sam. *"What do you think she was wearing?"*

*"I don't know,"* said Bob, *"But it sure needs ironing."*

———————————

**An old man** said to his friend, *"I wish I knew where I was going to die."*

*"Why would you want to know that?"* asked the friend.

*"So that I could avoid ever going there!"*

———————————

### *You Know You're Getting Old When....*

You read the obituaries each day to make sure you're not listed.

**After meeting on** a seniors' trip, a couple began dating. They enjoyed each other's company and after taking things slowly at first, their relationship began to heat up and get more physical. One evening after a romantic candlelight dinner and a bottle of wine, they ended up in bed together.

Afterwards, each was lost in their own thought. He was thinking, *"If I'd known she was a virgin, I'd have been more gentle."*

And she was thinking, *"If I'd known he could still get it up, I'd have taken off my tights."*

---

**A wife woke up** one morning and leaned over to give her husband an affectionate kiss.

*"Don't touch me!,"* he yelled, *"I'm dead!"*

*"What on earth are you talking about?"* said his wife. *"We're both awake so what makes you think you're dead?"*

*"I must be dead,"* he replied, *"because I woke up this morning and nothing hurts!"*

**An elderly man** went to his doctor and said: *"Doc, I think I'm getting senile. Several times lately, I have forgotten to zip up."*

*"That's not senility,"* replied the doctor. *"Senility is when you forget to zip down."*

━━━━━━━━━━━━━━━━

**Told that he** had just twenty-four hours to live, a man in his fifties decided to go home and make passionate love to his wife. He crept into the bedroom, slid into bed and for the next three hours enjoyed the wildest sex he had ever experienced. Finally exhausted, he crawled into the bathroom where he was surprised to find his wife lying in the bathtub with a mudpack on her face.

*"How did you get in here?"* he asked.

*"Sssh!"* she said. *"You'll wake my mother."*

**A wife arrived** home from her weekly shopping trip to find her ninety-six-year-old husband in bed with another woman. In a jealous rage, she pushed him off the balcony of their apartment and sent him tumbling to his death. She was charged with murder and at her trial the judge asked her whether there was anything she wanted to say by way of mitigation.

*"Well, Judge,"* she said coolly, *"I figured that at ninety-six, if he could make love to another woman, he could fly, too!"*

---

**An old lady fell** into the water and called for help. A man jumped in to save her and grabbed her by the hair but she was wearing a wig and it came off. He then grabbed her by the chin and her false teeth popped out. Frustrated the man then yelled, *"Somebody help me save all of this woman that we can!"*

**A eighty-two** year old man married a girl almost 60 years his junior. As he climbed into bed for the first time, he asked his bride, *"Did your mother tell you what to do on your wedding night?"*

*"Yes, she told me everything,"* replied the girl, kissing him gently.

*"Good,"* said the old man, turning out the light, *"because I've forgotten."*

---

**An elderly woman** was admitted to the hospital with a mystery illness. After monitoring her for two days, the doctor told her, *"You have acute angina."*

*"Oh, doctor,"* said the old woman blushing, *"you do say the sweetest things!"*

**A woman** was standing naked in front of the mirror. *"Look at me,"* she said sadly to her husband, *"I'm old and fat. Cheer me up by paying me a compliment."*
The husband replied: *"Your eyesight is still good."*

---

**Two old men** - John and Harry - were sitting quietly in a bar. *"When was the last time you made love to a woman?"* John asked Harry.
*"1955,"* replied Harry.
*"My goodness!"*, exclaimed John. *"That's a long time ago."*
*"Not really,"* said Harry, glancing at his watch. *"It's only twenty past eight now."*

---

*You Know You're Getting Old When....*

The little gray-haired lady you helped across the street is your wife.

**A husband and wife** were celebrating their 60th wedding anniversary and a newspaper reporter had been sent to cover the occasion.

*"You look remarkably healthy for your age,"* said the reporter.

The wife replied: *"I've never had one sick day in my entire life."*

*"So you've never been bedridden."* replied the reporter.

*"Oh, thousands of times!,"* she said. *"And twice in a golf buggy!"*

---

**A son hesitantly** asked his mother, *"I know it's an unpleasant subject but when you go, would you rather be cremated or buried?"*

*"Oh, I really don't care,"* replied the mother. *"Surprise me!"*

**A widow was** telling her grown daughter about a date she had with a 90 year old man. *"I had to slap his face four times in the course of the evening!"*

The daughter was horrified. *"The thought of him trying to get fresh with you at his age!"*

*"No, it wasn't that,"* explained the mother. *"I had to keep slapping his face to keep him awake."*

━━━━━━━━━━━━━━━━━━━━━

**To the envy** of his friends, a 76 year old man married a sexy 20 year old model.

*"You lucky devil"*, said one of his friends. *"How did you manage to land such a beautiful young wife?"*

*"Easy,"* replied the millionaire, *"I told her I was 98."*

# Senior Dating Ads

## In Good Condition

Male, 1929, high mileage, in good condition, some hair, many new parts including knees, cow heart valve, hip, cornea and more. I can usually remember Monday through Thursday. If you can remember Friday, Saturday and Sunday, let's get together!

## Serenity Now

I'm into solitude, long walks and meditation. If you are the silent type, let's get together, take our hearing aids out and enjoy quiet times.

## Foxy Lady

Blue-haired beauty, slim, 5'2" (use to be 5'4"), searching for sharp dressing companion. No soup stains on tie please.

**An old man** was a witness in a robbery case. The defense lawyer asked him, *"Did you see my client commit this robbery?"*

*"Yes, I did,"* said the old man.

*"Can you be absolutely certain that it was my client?"* continued the lawyer. *"Let's not forget, the robbery took place at night."*

*"I'm definitely sure it was him,"* said the old man. *"I got a good look at him."*

*"You may think you did,"* persisted the lawyer, *"but you are 88 years old and the suspect was standing on the other side of the street. Just exactly how far can you see - particularly at night?"*

*"Well,"* replied the old man, *"I can see the moon. Is that far enough for you?"*

---

### You Know You're Getting Old When....

You have too much room in the house and not enough in the medicine cabinet.

**An elderly man** boarded a crowded city bus but nobody would give him a seat. When the bus jerked away, the old man's walking stick slipped and he fell to the floor. As he got to his feet, a boy of about 10 sitting near him said, *"If you put a little rubber thing on the end of your stick, it wouldn't slip."*

The old man replied, *"Yes, son, and if your father had done the same thing 10 years ago, I'd have a seat on this bus today!"*

---

**A young girl** wondered why her grandfather needed three pair of glasses. *"I have one pair for my long sight and one pair for my short sight,"* he explained to her. *"The third pair is so I can look for the other two."*

**A 91 year old man** went to the doctor and said: *"Doctor, my sex drive is too high. I want it lowered."*

*"Am I hearing you right?"* asked the dumbfounded doctor. *"You're 91 and you want your sex drive lowered?"*

*"That's right,"* said the old man pointing to his head. *"It's all up here at the moment and I want it lowered."*

---

**Two old widows** were sitting in their nursing home and were talking about their late husbands when one turned to the other and said, *"Did you and your husband have mutual orgasms?"*

*"No,"* replied the other widow, *"I think we were with the Prudential."*

**A woman went** to the police to report her husband missing. She said, *"He's 50, six feet two inches tall, blue eyes, dark hair, athletic build, weighs about 180 pounds and is smartly dressed and softly spoken."* Her friend then protested, *"Your husband is five foot tall, has dark eyes, is overweight with a large beer gut, bald, and has a loud mouth!"*

*"I know,"* said the wife. *"But who wants him back?"*

━━━━━━━━━━━━━━━━━━

**A middle-aged couple** were discussing their future. The husband announced, *"When I'm 80, I intend to find myself a pretty 20 year old girl and have the time of my life."*

*"And when I'm 80,"* said his wife, *"I plan on finding myself a 20 year old hunk. And as you know, 20 goes into 80 a lot easier than 80 goes into 20!"*

**An old man** went to the doctor for a regular check-up. The doctor listened to his heart and declared, *"I'm afraid you have a serious heart murmur. Do you smoke at all?"*

*"No, doctor."*

*"Do you drink to excess?"*

*"No, doctor."*

*"Do you still have a sex life?"*

*"Yes, doctor."*

*"Well, I'm sorry to have to be the bearer of bad news, but with this heart murmur, you'll have to give up half of your sex life."*

*"Which half?"* asked the old man, *"the looking or the thinking?"*

---

### *You Know You're Getting Old When....*

You give up all of your bad habits
and you still don't feel good.

**A young man** asked a weathly old man how he had made his fortune. The old guy said, *"Well, son, it was back in 1932 at the height of the Great Depression. I was down to my last nickle so I invested my nickle in an apple. I spent the entire day polishing that apple and at the end of the day, I sold the apple for ten cents. The next morning, I invested that ten cents in two apples and polished them and then sold them for twenty cents. I continued this system for a month and by the end of the month, I had accumulated a fortune of $5.60. Then my wife's father died and left us two million dollars!"*

---

### *You Know You're Getting Old When....*

You turn out the lights for economic rather than romantic reasons.

# Memory Test

Three senior men were at the doctor's office for a memory test.

*"What is two times two?"* the doctor asked the first.

*"177,"* came the reply.

Then the doctor asked the second old man, *"What is two times two?"*

*"Wednesday,"* the man said.

The doctor then turned to the third old man and asked him, *"What is two times two?"*

*"Four,"* he answered.

*"That's excellent,"* enthused the doctor. *"How did you get that?"*

*"Easy",* said the third old man. *"I subtracted 177 from Wednesday."*

---

### *You Know You're Getting Old When....*

Your little black book contains

only names ending in MD.

**A couple** who had been married for 45 years were lying in bed one night in a motel. They were just about to go to sleep when they heard a woman's voice in the next room say, *"Oh, baby, you're so hot and strong."*

The husband then turned to his wife and said, *"Why don't you ever tell me that?"*

She then replied, *"Because you're not hot and strong any longer."*

A few minutes later they heard the girl's voice groan, *"Oh, baby, that was a wonderful orgasm. Thank you."*

The husband then turned to his wife and said, *"Why don't you ever tell me when you have a wonderful orgasm?"*

*"Because,"* she said, *"you're never around when I have them!"*

**After 55 years** of marriage, a couple were lying in bed one night when the husband started to fondle her in a passionate manner. His right hand started at her neck and made its way down her back with his fingers exploring every fold of skin. He then began to tenderly caress her breasts before stopping at her stomach. Next he gently rubbed her left buttock and placed his hand on her left inner thigh, moving down to feel her calf. He then transferred his hand to her other leg proceeding up her inner thigh until he reached the very top of her leg. Suddenly without warning he stopped and moved his hand away.

She had become very aroused by his caressing and said lovingly, *"Honey, that was wonderful. Why did you stop?"*

He responded, *"I just found the remote."*

**A doctor told an old lady** that in order to improve her heart rate that she would have to have sex three times a week. Embarrassed, she asked the doctor to go into the waiting room and repeat the suggestion to her husband. So the doctor went into the waiting room and told the husband that his wife needed to have sex three times a week.

*"Which days?"* asked the husband.

*"Well, something like Mondays, Wednesdays and Fridays would be ideal,"* said the doctor.

*"Okay, Doc,"* said the husband, *"I can get her here on Mondays and Wednesdays, but on Fridays she'll have to get here by a taxi."*

---

### *You Know You're Getting Old When....*

You feel like the morning after but you haven't been anywhere.

**A doctor entered** his examining room to find a woman and baby waiting for him. After examining the baby, the doctor revealed that he was concerned that it wasn't gaining enough weight. *"Is the baby breast-fed or bottle-fed?"* he asked. *"Breast-fed,"* replied the woman.

The doctor ordered the woman to strip down to her waist and he then proceeded to knead and pinch both of her breasts. Motioning her to get dressed, he said, *"No wonder this baby is hungry. You don't have any milk."*

*"I know,"* she said, *"I'm his grandmother but I'm so glad I came!"*

---

*You Know You're Getting Old When....*

You put your bra on back to front
and it fits better.

**An elderly lady** from the country was visiting the city for the first time in her life. She checked in at a hotel and then let a porter take her bags. She followed him and as the doors closed, there was a look of disgust on her face.

*"Young man,"* she said angrily, *"I may be old and not use to big city ways but I'm not stupid. I paid good money for this room and it won't do at all. It's way too small, has no windows or proper ventilation, and doesn't even have a bed!"*

*"Madam,"* replied the porter, *"this isn't your room.......you're in an elevator!"*

---

### *You Know You're Getting Old When....*
Your investment in health insurance is finally beginning to pay off.

**A middle aged** man sat at a bar and ordered a double vodka. He drank it, looked inside his jacket pocket and ordered another double vodka. When he had finished that drink, he looked inside his jacket pocket again and ordered another double vodka.

Puzzled by this routine, the bartender asked him, *"Why do you look inside your jacket pocket every time you order a drink?"*

*"I'm looking at a photo of my wife,"* replied the man. *"When she starts to look good, I know it's time to go home."*

---

### *You Know You're Getting Old When....*

You remember when the only people who wore rings in their noses were pygmies.

**An elderly couple** had been dating for over eight years and finally decided it was time to get married. But they first wanted to work out the details of how their marriage was going to work in order to avoid any misunderstandings or disappointments.

So over dinner they had a long conversation about their future. They discussed finances, living arrangements and all manner of things that affected them both. The old man took written notes of every point they covered. Finally he thought he should mention the physical side of their relationship.

*"How do you feel about sex?"* he asked tentatively, pencil in hand.

*"Well,"* replied the old lady, choosing her words carefully, *"I'd have to say I would like it infrequently."*

The old man then inquired, *"Is that one word or two?"*

**An elderly rancher** had just married a sexy girl of 23. His good friend, the town mayor, was concerned about how long the old man would be able to satisfy such a young bride and feared that the marriage might quickly disintegrate. So he advised the rancher to recruit a hired hand to help around the place, knowing full well that the hired hand would probably help out in the bedroom, too, behind the old man's back.

To the mayor's relief, the rancher thought it was a great idea.

A few months later, the mayor called on his friend again and asked, *"How's your new wife?"*

*"She's pregnant,"* replied the old man.

The mayor smiled knowingly. *"And how's the hired hand?"*

*"Oh, she's pregnant too!"*

**An elderly couple** were watching a healing service on TV. The evangelist proclaimed that anyone who wanted to be healed should place one hand on the TV set and the other hand on the affected body part.

Slowly the old lady got to her feet, tottered over to the TV, placed her right hand on the set and her left hand on the arthritic shoulder that had been causing her such pain.

Then the old man got up, made his way over to the TV, placed his right hand on the set and his left hand on his crotch.

*"What do you think you're doing?"* snapped his wife. *"The idea is to heal the sick, not raise the dead!"*

**Shortly before his death,** an elderly man instructed his wife, "*When I die, I want you to put all my money into the coffin with me. I've worked hard to earn that money, and I want to take it to the after life with me.*"

So on the day of his funeral, just before the coffin was lowered into the ground, the wife asked the undertaker to open the lid.

Her friend said, "*Surely you're not going to go along with the old miser's last request?*"

The wife said, "*I'm a woman of my word.*"

The lid was opened and the wife pushed in a large envelope in accordance with the deceased's wishes.

"*You must be crazy!*" said the friend. "*I did what I promised,*" replied the wife. "*I got all of his money together, put it in my account and wrote him a check. If he can cash it, he can spend it!*"

**An elderly woman** visited the doctor with a list of complaints about her deteriorating health. Her joints were stiff, her back ached, her vision was on the decline and she had a weak bladder.

*"I'm afraid,"* said the doctor, *"you have to accept the fact that as you get older things will start to go downhill. After all, who wants to live to a hundred?"*

The woman replied, *"Anyone who's ninety-nine."*

---

**A 89 year old man** married a 26 year old woman and took her on a honeymoon to Bermuda. When he returned, his brother asked him how it had gone. *"Oh, it was wonderful,"* he said. *"We made love almost every night." "That's quite a feat at your age,"* replied his brother. *"Yes,"* he continued, *"Almost on Monday, almost on Tuesday, almost on Wednesday . . . "*

**A man in his seventies** returned from the doctor and told his wife that he was terminally ill and had only twenty hours to live. In view of this bad news, he asked his wife for sex and she readily agreed and they made love. Six hours later he said to his wife, *"Dearest, you know I have only fourteen hours to live. Could we please have sex one more time?"* She agreed and they made love again.

That evening as he climbed into bed, he tapped his wife on the shoulder and said, *"please honey just one more time because I only have eight more hours before I die."* *"Okay,"* she said, and they made love again for a third time. Four hours later, he woke her from a deep sleep and said, *"I only have four more hours to live. How about we have sex one last time?"* *"Listen,"* she snapped, *"I have to get up in the morning - you don't!"*

**At a family gathering** a young boy decided to play a trick on his grandfather by putting a Viagra tablet in his drink. After a while, his Grandfather excused himself to go to the bathroom. When he returned, the front of his pants was wet all over.

*"What happened?"* asked his grandson.

*"Well,"* said his grandfather, *"I had to go take a leak but when I took it out and saw that it wasn't mine, I put it back in again."*

---

### *You Know You're Getting Old When....*

You stop half way up the stairs and can't remember if you were going up or coming down.

**After hearing of** the death of her grandfather, the young woman went to comfort her grieving grandmother.

*"How did grandad die,"* she asked her grandmother.

*"He had a heart attack Sunday morning while we were making love."*

*"Isn't it risky to have sex at your age?"* asked the granddaughter.

*"No, not really. We decided to make love only once a week and to the sound of church bells. They have just the right rhythm which is nice and slow and even. Nothing too strenuous. However, your grandfather would still be alive today if that ice cream truck hadn't gone by."*

---

### *You Know You're Getting Old When....*

You have a party and the neighbors don't even realize it.

**A woman goes** to a doctor who tells her she only has one month to live and that the bill will be $1,000. The woman replies that there is no way that she can pay the bill before the end of the month. The doctor then says, *"Okay then, I'll give you six months to live."*

---

**The nurse explained** to an old man in the hospital that the law requires that patients have an opportunity to make decisions about their own care. *"Do you have any suggestions for ways we can make you more comfortable, Sir,"* she said. *"Yes,"* he said, *"Pour a cup of scotch down my feeding tube, destroy the little black book in my drawer, and call my malpractice attorney!"*

---

**You show me** a man that says he can do at 50 what he did at 25 and I'll show you a man who didn't do much at 25.

**There were two** old gentlemen who lived in a retirement home and spent a lot of time together. They went out to eat, took walks to their stock broker's office and played golf. Then one of them became very *"down"* and the other could not manage to get him to talk about what was wrong. Finally, after several weeks of questioning him, he responded, *"I'm so ashamed. Would you believe I have VD at 89?"* His friend responded, *"That's not so bad, I have IBM at 72."*

---

**An old man** sees a friend sitting on a park bench weeping. *"How have things been with you Tom,"* he asks his friend. *"Great",* Tom says. *"I just married a beautiful young woman."* *"Wonderful! But then why are you crying?"* Tom replies, *"I can't remember where I live!"*

**A very healthy,** spry-looking 94-year old man moves into a nursing home. He walks up to a frail looking man walking down the hall with a walker and says, *"How old do you think I am?"* The man answers, *"I'd say 60."* *"No, I'm 94!"*, the man boasts. Down the hall, he sees a woman in a room watching TV from a wheelchair and walks up to her and asks her to guess his age. Right away she unzips his fly and fondles him for a few minutes, then looks at him and says, *"You're 94."* The man looks at her incredulously and asks, *"How did you know that?"* She shrugs and says, *"I heard you tell the fellow in the hall."*

---

**Seniors are worth** a fortune. They have silver in their hair, gold in their teeth, stones in their kidneys and gallbladder, lead in their feet, and gas in their stomach.

**Do you know** the four signs of growing old? **1.** Forgetting names. **2.** Forgetting faces. **3.** Forgetting to zip up. **4.** Forgetting to zip down.

---

**Two old ladies** were rocking in their chairs on the nursing home porch. One says, *"Betty, do you remember the minuet?"* Betty answers, *"Heck, I don't remember the ones I slept with."*

---

**Two old men** sitting in rockers on the front porch of rest home when a young lady walks by wearing a mini skirt. Bill says, *"Joe you see that?" "Yeah, I do Bill, she's mighty nice."* Bill replies, rocking fast, *"I would like to take her out, wine and dine her, and.......*(rocking slowing down)....*Joe, what's that other thing we used to do."*

---

**The nice thing** about being senile...you are always meeting new friends!

# Other Books by
# Pearce W. Hammond

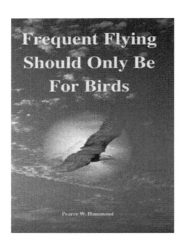

**"Frequent Flying Should Only Be For Birds "**
If you are a Frequent Flyer or an In-Frequent Flyer, this humorous book about flying is for you. The author spent many hours in the air as a Frequent Flyer and earned the right to write this book which contains humorous chapters on: You know you're a frequent flyer when....; Frequent Flyer Dictionary; Quotes about flying; Airway Rules; Airline Obituaries; Flight Attendant Humor; and Flying Jokes.

**Paperback     2013     ISBN 9781482004229**

Available online from: *www.pearcehammond.com and from Amazon.com and other book retailers.*

# Other Books by
# Pearce W. Hammond

## "Listen To Me"

This book gives a humorous glimpse into the lives of dogs from their point-of-view and answers many of the questions that have been "dogging" humans for years, such as: Can dogs write poetry? Do dogs have wisdom? What do they think about during the day? Can people learn from dogs, and much, much more. This book is a must-read for every dog owner and dog lover who wants to experience the therapeutic effects of laughing.

**Paperback     2011     ISBN 9781461132790**
**Library of Congress Control Number: 2011913752**

Available online from:*www.pearcehammond.com and from Amazon.com and other book retailers.*

# Other Books by Pearce W. Hammond

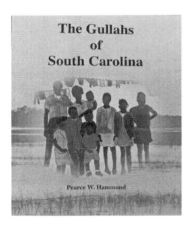

## "The Gullahs of South Carolina"

This book tells an important story about the Gullah people of South Carolina and their vanishing way of life and culture. The book is illustrated with the author's original paintings and creates public awareness of the unique Gullah language, lifestyle and culture so that future generations will know and recognize the significant contributions the Gullah people have made to South Carolina and to America's heritage.

**Paperback     2011     ISBN 9780615486482**
**Library of Congress Control Number: 2011929319**

Available online from:*www.pearcehammond.com*
*and from Amazon.com and other book retailers.*

Made in the USA
San Bernardino, CA
10 March 2014